Dearest Lovem
thank you for your support
and best wishes

18/12/2020

LOOKING OUT AT THE WORLD
THROUGH POETRY

HERBIE DUNNAN

authorHOUSE®

AuthorHouse™ UK
1663 Liberty Drive
Bloomington, IN 47403 USA
www.authorhouse.co.uk
Phone: UK TFN: 0800 0148641 (Toll Free inside the UK)
        UK Local: 02036 956322 (+44 20 3695 6322 from outside the UK)

Published by AuthorHouse 09/24/2020

ISBN: 978-1-7283-7906-7 (sc)
ISBN: 978-1-7283-7907-4 (hc)
ISBN: 978-1-7283-7905-0 (e)

DEDICATIONS

This book is dedicated to all key workers who have tirelessly kept us going during this pandemic, key workers who we've lost, losing, or will lose in the future because of it. Hospital workers, all school workers, shop workers, street cleaners etc, you have all been invaluable to the cause.

ACKNOWLEDGMENT

Writing this book has given me the opportunity to say an everlasting thank you to a few people who have supported me and guided me throughout this campaign.

First of all I would like to say a big thank you to my illustrator, Tracey Bacchus; for your brilliant art work which you've completed under extreme pressure.

Gabriella Medina Noa, I work with you everyday you make it a pleasure to come to work; you are my boss, but you give me freedom to express myself, this makes it a happy place to work.

Victoria Bond, my friend from way back; thank you for your input contribution and encouraging me when my brain seized up.

Paulette Campbell, thank you for your encouragement and know how it has been invaluable.

My brother-in-law Ronald Griffith, thank you for your contribution, the decision was hard but I had to make a choice.

Ashley Porter, last but not least; my trainer and mentor, without your training and good words I might not have been able to continue, you prove exercise with knowledge is a wonderful thing.

CONTENTS

LOOKING OUT AT THE WORLD

Looking out on the world it all seems so scary
You try to be positive, but life is quite dreary.
You try to be optimistic but there's so many setbacks
Sometimes it's colourful and there's nothing you lack

However, there are people suffering; and no one trying to help
People being selfish just thinking about themselves
Children dying all over the world; dying of starvation,
Countries killing people just to make an acquisition

Terrorists blowing up and killing innocent people
Why do they do this? For their own depraved reason.
Young people killing each other just to get a status
When is it all going to stop? This is so outrageous

If we could all live as one and look out for each other
The world would be a better place I'm sure this we'd discover
Let's all live as one and make a better place
Help one another and save the human race.

POLITICAL

As I get older, I'm becoming more political
Talking about things that happened; historical.
How we've been treated; physical,
How many have died? Numerical.

The colour of my skin is embedded with melanin,
Be proud to be black; the youths I'm empowering,
Racism is vast this is concerning,
Teach our history in schools; this will help with the learning.

As I get older and become more political
I look at things; I get sentimental,
If things don't get better, it could be detrimental
Thinking about it I get quite emotional.

We try to emancipate, but they won't cooperate
They won't listen to our debate.
So now this just frustrates; and aggravate
The corners of our minds, so in their heads we try to penetrate.

HOW I DID IT

I decided to write a book
I was encouraged to do so,
I jotted down things on pieces of paper
To see how far it would go,

I made notes of anything that came to my head
Things that I observed be- it alive or dead.
I liked the thought of writing, it made me feel free
But now it's hard to stop and that's what worrying me.

I write about this and that
Things that make me happy or sad,
Things that make me laugh
And things that made me mad.

I like to see my work in print
It's a lovely feeling,
I like to speak my mind
My thoughts I am revealing

KILLING ON THE STREETS

Every day we hear the same thing
Another murder another killing,
It maybe a shooting maybe a stabbing
But someone's dead or they're dying.

Are you doing this to gain street cred?
But who knows? you may soon be dead,
I walk on the street where it's red
It's the spot where another's bled.

Every day we hear blam, blam, blam,
Now police hunting another gun man.
How many black youths left in the city?
Not a lot and oh what a pity.

Non - blacks are laughing; at us killing our own
You're not giving our own time to grow.

Every day we hear the same thing
Another murder another killing
Turn on the TV and hear the news,
Another family's child has been abused.

Where did you get your gun?
Where did you get your knife?
Look what you've done
You have ruined another family's life.

You are killing people and don't want anyone to snitch
All you are doing is making the florist rich.
We're walking on the street looking over our shoulder,
When is this war going to be over?

Every day we hear the same thing
Another murder another killing,
It maybe a shooting it maybe a stabbing
But someone's dead or they're dying.

WIND RUSH CRISIS

(Give me a passport)
Give me a passport give it for free
Bout you standing there interrogating me
Give me a passport give it now
Stop all the nonsense about wind rush row.

You took us from our land and yard
We come here and we work hard
We build up your country for little pay
Now you tell us we can't stay.

Give me a passport give it for free
Why are you chatting bout deporting me?

BRITISH PASSPORT

WINDRUSH

THE CUP IS NOT COMING HOME

The street is now filled
With discarded flags,
Discarded banners
Discarded mags.

Discarded pint glasses
Lay on wet floors,
The joy of England reaching
The final is gone once more.

Oh yes, they played well
And did us all proud,
But it's goals that win matches
Not cheers from the crowd.

THE CORPSE IN MY FLAT

There's a corpse in my flat it's laying on the floor
It's lying on its back not breathing any more
It came through the window it came in unannounced
So, the minute I saw it I pounced.

It moved quite fast and hid behind the curtain
What was behind there? I'm not certain
So, I went to the cupboard and took my weapon out
When it showed its head again, I pounced

When I took off the cover, and pressed, it went hiss
My aim was good I just could not miss.
It wriggled and wriggled then sped up fast
But I was sure it would die; it would not last

It dropped to the floor then landed on its back
Should I just leave it or give it a whack?
The corpse on the floor it came in to die
I just can't stand these awful flies.

THE TOTTENHAM PLAN

For years the cabinet's been empty
We've tried but we've failed,
But Mauricio Pochettino
Is getting us out of jail.

His attitude his authority
His humour and his style
His enthusiasm makes us better by miles.

We've got a new stadium
The best in the land oh I wish I could afford
A seat that would be grand

Now they've sacked Mauricio and installed Jose
He is a proven winner; well that's what they say
We'll have to see how; it all works out
The game's about winning and we've won nought.

THEY'VE GONE

The 15th of June we finally said goodbye
It was emotional but I saw no one cry
It's been a turbulent year; you know this I won't lie
We've had our ups and downs but now we've said bye-bye

Berat- the joker a very funny guy
Kell- the ladies' man he's not shy
Turan- the want to be gangster but he just hasn't got it in him
Aka Grimz but I know not for what reason.

Naomi- the lip gloss queen; you're prettier than you think
When guys look at you, they always give you a wink.
Justina- you are gorgeous keep doing your
art; please don't get distracted
Don't let it fall apart.

Natasha- with your beauty you can do no wrong
Just try to be happy, positive and strong.
Samir- I think you're creative and give everything
Your personal touch; we'll miss you all so much.

The lovely **Mrs Medina** has done an awful lot
She's helped you all to understand
So, you didn't lose the plot.
And there's little old me just plodding along
Maybe I'll write another book and include you lot; or better still a song.

PROBLEM IN THE HOSPITAL

I'm sitting in the hospital waiting patiently;
What have I done wrong? Why are they avoiding me?
I see people come and go doctors and nurses too,
I'm nowhere knowing what's wrong I haven't got a clue.

They call out names like
Sanjay, Gustav, Winston and Joe
They haven't called mine yet
So, I just don't know.

The parking is abysmal
And it cost the earth
So, I risked parking on a side road
For what it's bloody worth.

Matt Hancock the new health secretary
I wonder what he's going to do.
Hope he's better than the last one,
Because he messed it up and then flew.

MY PARENTS

Every day I think of my parents
Although they have been gone for years,
I think of what they would have thought of me now
And yes; I have had to hold back tears.

I hope they would be proud of me
I know they were hard to please,
Sometimes we seemed so different,
Just like chalk and cheese.

But I always showed them honesty and respect
Never tried to upset them; well not direct
Manners and respect that's what we were taught
If we didn't follow we would have felt their wrath.

WATER!

Water known as H2 O is very good for you
Drink it in the morning and the whole day through,
It flushes out your kidneys and de-tox your internal organs
It's important you drink it daily it helps stop dehydration.

Water helps to maximize physical performance,
Drinking water, will increase your endurance.
It helps to; stimulate your brain,
Keeps it hydrated, stops you going insane.

Water helps, to relive constipation,
It really does help with your bodily function.
Drinking water may help, to treat kidney stones,
Stops urinary infections and strengthen your bones.

INDECISIVE

From I've know you you've been indecisive
You don't really know what you want,
You change your mind at the drop of a hat
You say I will then I can't.

You're always trying to fix things
Even If they're not broken,
I don't understand your train of thought
Your true thoughts is never spoken.

THE PLANT

I took a plant from my place of work
That someone had brought in,
It's been there for years slowly decaying.

The owner left; and it decayed even further,
I thought I would take it home.
Or should I really bother?

The plan was to save it from its imminent doom,
But I think it was too late
Now I look at it with gloom.

I have decided to read up about it
To see if I can inject,
Some new life into it to see what I can get.

The original owner, was a lovely lady
Named Ann, a wonderful kind person
So, you understand?

I hope the plant will thrive again I hope to resurrect it,
If there was a serum, I could buy
I would gladly buy and inject it.

DREAMS

Dreams can be good it can also be bad
It can make you happy but can also make you sad
It's your mind working while you're asleep
They can be quite intense; very deep

Dreams can be funny frightening and strange
It's something you can't determine
Or even prearrange

Dreams can clear your mind
Can also make you confused
Make you scared and cry
Or make you feel amused

They have dreams they call nightmares
Now they are scary
Be careful what you eat before you go to sleep
Yes, you must be ready.

Woke up feeling bad this morning
So, I decided to go to the gym
Had a workout, steam and sauna
I also had a swim.

Feeling much better now I'm
Walking down the street
A woman in front of me vaping
Her smoke was not discrete

So now my lungs are engulfed
In smoke, I thought what the heck?
It may not be nicotine but its
Still going down my neck.

If I went and shouted in her ear
I doubt if she would like that
I'd be invading her space;
Like she has mine, and that would not be appropriate

So, give consideration for those nearby
When you do whatever you do
Think of what you're doing and why.
Don't do to others if you wouldn't like it done to you.

BHM

Black history month has come around again
But I'm not really impressed
Why are we learning about black history only for a month?
This I can't digest

We discover great things blacks have done
And focus on them that's true,
But why is it only for a month?
I haven't got a clue.

We aspire to achieve equality
To make the youngsters aware
But we're not teaching it each week
It seems there's some kind of fear.

I understand its English schools
And English should be taught,
But in history lessons; include black history
Don't leave the children short.

Knowledge is power so why are we
Stopping them from knowing?
If the truth be told we should be bold
I believe it would help their growing.

The youths don't know where they come from
Or what's gone on in the past
They only learn about Macbeth, King Arthur,
Jason and the Argonauts

So, while you're having fun
Don't think about it just for today
Think about a weekly intervention
On black history; in the long run it will pay.

A1_FLEEKY AND A1_CHINKS

a1_fleeky and a1_chinks sisters so supreme
a1_fleeky entrepreneur she really is the cream
She works hard and studies too; she's aiming for the top,
She wants to be the crème De la crème and she'll work until she drops.

Little sister chinks she's studying too; but she's got some way to go
She too will also succeed; her determination shows
They're eager to reach the top no matter what it takes
These two girls are great they won't give you heartache

Mama you must be so proud of your girls; the apple of your eye,
Your beautiful black pearls, they want to make you happy
For all you've done for them, they see you as a mother
Also, as a friend

You may have thought they were going to be trouble
But they've grown and burst that bubble
I'm sure they will be great,
Sisters together they can't be beat

a1_fleeky and a1_chinks these two sisters are on the brink
posing and strutting their stuff, taking selfies they look buff.

SISTER @ SIXTY

You're sixty years old and I've got to say wow!
My little sister is a big woman now.
Siblings from birth we haven't always seen eye to eye,
But our blood will be the same until the day we die.

Memories of growing up has stuck in my mind,
We we're brought up properly to be considerate and kind.
You've been through a lot with your personal situation,
But you've come through it bravely you're a sensation.

I wish Mum and Dad were here to see,
What a good job they've done raising us three.
So, it fills me with pride to say,
Very best wishes happy birthday.

ECONOMY OR LIFE?

So, is it about the economy or is it about life?
Restaurant and pubs opening; it's causing some strife,
Beaches are packed this is a danger
We won't be able to stop mingling with strangers.

Four months we have waited we thought it would pass
But the virus, is still kicking ass,
Don't go to work, go to work now
Take public transport, don't take public transport; wow!

GREAT BLACK MEN

Some great black men are dying, assassinated I'm not lying
All because they're trying to tell the world the truth.
Why can't we all see they don't want you or me,
They want to keep us, down in poverty.

Some will say that they're doing us good
And it looks good on paper,
But let's look beyond, their handshake
And signature.

If they're giving us anything at all there's more in it for them
They're raping our women and killing our black men
They are taking not giving and throwing us crumbs,
We need to check this out, it makes me feel numb.

LIFT UP YOURSELF

You always seem to focus on bad decisions that you make,
You've made a lot of good ones too so don't underestimate.
Don't put yourself down or beat yourself up be proud and believe,
If you do make mistakes just start again and roll up your sleeve.

THE PAIN IN MY BODY

The pain in my body is getting me down so I feel I've got to say,
M y thoughts and feelings; to you I must convey.
Through no fault of my own I was knocked down and yes, I survived,
I'm thankful to the lord for saving me; I know I could have died.

Now it's the aftercare that's killing me I just don't understand,
The medical system is so confusing it seems
there's no one in command.
No one tells you what is wrong they just say take this pill,
Three months down the line; guess what I'm still I'll

So, you start to ask yourself am I really in pain?
But when the pain strikes you know you're not going insane,
Restriction of movement makes you feel confined, you feel like a cripple
And like you're going out of your mind.

It might seem good to be off work but it's sending me loco,
They listen and empathise but there's nothing at all to show.
They can't tell you what to do or help you with your feelings,
So basically, you've wasted your time and they've left you reeling.

I'm writing this at 3 in the morning because I cannot sleep,
The pain has got me again, if I don't write I will weep.

THAT DAY

That day in 2018 is a day I would like to forget,
But it plays around in my mind and gets me so upset.
A bright October morning about half past eight,
I was walking across a zebra crossing and a car hit me straight.

Without any warning it just came out the blue,
Yes, I did see it coming but there was nothing I could do.
The driver looked at me as I was halfway across,
It seems the car sped up fast and, in the air, I was tossed.

Lying on the ground was a humiliating experience,
Questions being asked they want to take my paticulars.
But my nose and mouth are bleeding I can hardly speak,
My body is shivering and I'm feeling weak.

I could hear sirens going and people sounding so alarmed,
All I'm thinking about is I'm cold; I want to be warm.
Silver blankets thrown over me this is a sensation
Anyone would think I'd just won the London marathon.

My shoulders are hurting, and I can see blood,
People saying to me you'll be alright love.
You'll be ok in a minute just a few details to check
But there's a pain in my shoulder and in my flaming neck.

I could hear Richard Woodall, Lita and Jen,
Leyla brought the blankets and our PC woman.
These are voices I remember; the ambulance lady too,
They want to call my partner how can I
remember; the number out the blue?

They're taking me to North Middlesex Hospital'
That's where my parents passed; I'm thinking
will I be ok or is this also my last?
But Lita is in the ambulance with me keeping my spirits up,
Giving me bare jokes and keep telling me I'm tough.

Waiting in A&E is like an eternity;
Do they even know I'm here are they coming to see me?
When they finally arrived, there was no speed in their approach
They just took it in their stride is this a joke.

Now they're asking the same questions that I've answered before
They're asking me what happened. I can't take this anymore.
My lips are bleeding and swollen I really cannot be asked to speak,
I 'm thinking I can't wait for this to be over
I'll be back to work in a week.

Nineteenth of October until today and I'm still not mended,
I'm still back and forth between three hospitals
when will this all be ending?
In the New Year I'm hoping for success and things will be better,
I'm hoping to get back to work; when? That doesn't really matter.

The fact is I'm still around; it could have been much worse,
So, thanks to everyone that helped and those who just observed.

LOCTICTIAN (BLAQUE TO NATURAL)

It's not just a place I go to get my hair done
It is a communal place I go to have fun.
Kadian happily meets me there,
She's the only one that does my hair.

She washes it and conditions it too
We talk nuff talk about things to do
Once a month I come down here
This is the place to be I swear.

Nuff people want locks it's not surprising
Natural culture it's an uprising
Young boys want to wear it some parents say no
I say leave them alone and let locks grow

It's not just a place I come to get my hair done
It's a communal place I go to have fun
Blaque to Natural is the place to be
They sort out my locks give me identity.

THE BOYS

My thoughts were with Diana
When I saw them walking in,
The new duke of Sussex
And the one who will be king

She would have been so happy
She would have smiled with glee,
She would have been so proud
Of Megan and Harry.

THE TAG ON MY FOOT

The tag on my foot was put there by law,
All because I broke someone's jaw.
The tag on my foot was put there to say,
You've done this so you'll have to pay.

My temper got the better of me
He took me to the limit,
He wanted some I gave him some
Yes, I'm the one that did it.

I'm under curfew; my time on the street is limited
My life is changing I feel it's been edited.
I'm thinking I must make changes,
My biography has too many bad pages.

The tag on my foot is making me think about life
Would I be the same if I had a family life?

A NEW YEAR (2020)

A new year a new start
Let's look forward and open our hearts.
Let's be positive another year has gone,
Hope 2020 is full of fun.

Some make resolutions
Hoping to carry them through
Out with the old in with the new
Praying all their dreams come true.

At twelve the bell tolls; everyone's cheering,
Thanking the lord for a new beginning.
Kissing, cuddling and saying cheers
So, from me HAPPY NEW YEAR!

OLDER

I sit alone and I reflect on my life and what could have been
Thought I'd be married by now, but it's been all a dream.
I've always been a gentleman always been polite
Always treated woman with respect, thought that would be alright.

As I get older, I feel more pain, I think about my life again
I think of what could have been; now I reminisce about things I've seen
In my life have I done good? What I wanted or what I could?
Have I listened and understood?

I've always worked one job or more I'm not rich but I'm not poor
It's hard to find a balance in life; what is bad and what is right
Is my life a success? I believe in God, so I know I'm blessed
I pray each day and It's so warming; God in my life Is so calming

I tried to be the man mummy and daddy wanted
But on the streets, there was so much hatred,
Look after yourself and stand firm,
The street way to earn respect I learned.

Yes, we're all aging fast, we look to the future
But think of the past.

END'S WAR

What end are you from? You're asking me
If you were from these ends, then you'd know "G"
Why you want to know? And what if I'm not?
You got something for me? You've lost the plot.

What ends am I from? Do you own this place?
You don't even pay tax; get out of my face,
What ends am I from? Do you really want to know?
Do you own these ends? Show me the proof bro.

You're asking me questions just like the feds
If I don't respond; what? You're goanna kill me dead?
I'm black you're black we're both the same
What is your problem? What is your game?

Have you ever had a job? Does your parent even work?
What gives you the right to ask these questions? Jerk!
You carry a knife; to try and intimidate,
You'll use it on anyone you don't discriminate.

I'm not scared of you and your sort; I don't even rate you
Out of ten I give you naught.
You are wearing your hood up in this bright sunshine
That's how smart you are; bout you committing crime.

BREXIT

I am not impressed with this Brexit mess, all this stuff I can't digest
Brexit is driving me insane it's on the news over and over again
Some say it's good some say it's bad this up and down
In and out is driving me mad

First of all why did we want to leave? The
whole country has been deceived
More money for our hospitals? Our borders will be ours?
No one checked out the implications, now they're not sure

If it wasn't broken why try to fix it
They've really messed it up with this bloody Brexit

MAMA'S 100TH BIRTHDAY

Happy birthday Mama one hundred; I'm happy and sad,
Hope you're celebrating in heaven and enjoying it with my Dad.
If you were still on earth the Queen would recognise this fact,
She would have sent you a telegram and we
would have all been proud of that.

Still each day you're never forgotten you're forever in our hearts
We miss you so dearly since the day from our life you depart.
We have happy memories of you and from time to time we reminisce,
It fills our hearts with laughter happiness and bliss.

We'll always love you Mama! Children,
grandchildren and great grandchildren too,
We'll talk about you forever that much I know is true.

1919-1920 RIP HAPPY BIRTHDAY

CROSSING THE ROAD

Like the Beatles I crossed the road on a Zebra,
Crossing the road should have been familiar
But a car hit me and nearly put me in the chiller
If it wasn't for the Lord, the driver would have been a killer

Give me strength because I'm hurting
If it wasn't for the Lord I'd be gone for certain,
Not enough witnesses no-one reporting
Forgive me father but for this I'm cursing.

No one wants to say exactly what happened
CCTV they say not working
What they did see they erased or something,
All this confusion is causing nuff fretting.

Surely, they can see I'm the victim
My life in front of me seem to be waning
Can't get no satisfaction like Mick Jagger said,
Maybe they all wish I was dead.

But I'm a fighter and I'll fight my corner
Though I'm waning I'll fight to be stronger
Then I'll fight this good and proper.
How can I show them how much I'm disgusted?
I want questions answered; nothing's done and dusted.

IN MY MIND

My mind tells me I'm young; each day it says you're twenty-one,
Even though I look much older my body's strong.
When I was younger, I wanted to be old, look older and do older things,
But now times moved on I see my age flying like it has wings.

I've never taken life for granted I look, and I observe
I try to look after my mind and body to give
the ageing process the swerve.
I do try to make the most of my life and give out a helping hand
But even at my age there are things I don't understand.

We're put on this earth for a reason for more reason than one
No one lives for eternity when your time comes, you're done.
So, if my mind keeps saying twenty-one and my body says you're not
Who am I to argue? That's the end of that.

DEAD MAN TALKING

I was walking in the park minding my own business
When I was approached and interrogated,
By a younger who looked and chat like me
An argument it seems he wanted, so an argument we formulated.

He asked me about what ends I was from
And who was my friends?
He told me round here he was the Don

He asked me; did I smoke weed?
When I said no, he didn't believe,
I told him to back off and leave me alone
That's when he tried to grab my phone.

I held on tight and gave him a kick
He took out his knife and gave me a slit
I took out my blade and we both struggled
I felt a sharp pain and in a heap we huddled.

He took out his phone and dialled 999
And then he ran away from the scene of the crime.
I'm losing my hearing I'm losing my sight
My body's shaking will I be alright?

There's a hole in my side I'm all alone
Is anyone coming to take me home?
It's all going dark and I'm really scared
God help me I feel weird.

Am I going to die or am I dead?
Someone help me please I beg,
I'm very cold and everything is white
It was all dark but now it's bright.

I feel calm and at peace
The whole in my side has gone I feel a release
I must be dead I'm sure I am
He took my life but destroyed my fam

Well it was me or him; couldn't we have sorted it out?
Without the blades being pulled out?
That's what happens if you walk with a knife
You're going to lose yours or take someone's life.

Mama's bawling sisters too
My life is over; what are they going to do?

YOUR DAUGHTER AIYANA

Your daughter is a bit of heaven and now she's here on earth
A vision of perfection ever since her birth.
A beautiful black rose that opens in the morn
Love her comfort her and always keep her warm.

She's a miracle, that makes you sit and wonder
Hope she will always lift you up, and never put you under.
She's like playing Mozart on an expensive grand piano
She's a beautiful princess and you gave her the name Aiyana.

MY MENTOR

My boxing coach is my mentor; he's forty I am sixty-three
But we get on well; like father and like son and that makes me happy,
He puts me through my paces, I'm now doing the old one two
I do hook jab slip and cross, we do healthy talking too

I also learn other things from him though I'm the older one,
The way he goes calmly about his business is really second to none
Everyone I know respects him they come to him for advice
He may be young but the old head on his
shoulders will make him immortalised

I've never heard him raise his voice shouting is not his thing
Though I've seen him separate fighters he calmly just wades in
His name is Ashley Porter his name should be on the centre
He gets my vote as north London's number one mentor.

IMAGINE

John Lennon asked us to imagine living our life in peace
He asked for all the anger in life to be decreased.
He thought he was a dreamer, but that's what he had on his mind
The world could be a much better place, but we must fix mankind.

STREETS OF TOTTENHAM

Have you seen the young boys walking up the high road?
They all have their hoods up their face hidden from view,
No one will employ them this is what destroys them
So, they all get angry dazed and confused

A policeman approach them tries to torment them
They get irritable because they feel abused
There's a lot of shouting a lot of bad mouthing
Someone's going to get battered and bruised.

MARRIAGE

Marriage is a decision that two people make,
Showing each other that all others they forsake.
You've been together for a while and the two of you are sure
That the love you have together; you both want more.

You're happy and you are content
And want to make your future brighter
Together you will make it work
And make any burden lighter.

I wish for you the very best
And hope your marriage succeed
You'll embrace good times and bad
Because that's what marriage needs.

Girls and boys, I wish for you happiness and pleasure
Just thank the Lord above because he gave you each other.

CHANGES

Rivers that used to be full, are now running dry,
Have you ever asked the question; why?
Times are changing, let's check ourselves,
The rich getting richer but that's only finical wealth.

What will they gain or will it last?
God's love is forever it will never pass,
So much foretold in the Bible is happening now,
We should all take heed and not just say wow!

Don't be amazed it's there to be read
Things that's happening now it's already been said.
Prayers is the answer he's waiting for you
Don't just sit back and ask, what's the world coming to.

THINGS MY PARENTS USE TO SAY

If you play with fire you will get burn
These are the things young people must learn
Who won't hear will certainly feel,
Take it on board this is for real.

What goes around comes around; these words are true and sound
Do unto others as you would like others do unto you
In life these words will get you through
Don't act too big for your boots, always remember your roots.

Look before you leap if you jump it could be deep
How you land could make you weep.
If the chicken is merry the hawk is near
If you're too happy you'd better take care

Two wrongs don't make a right; think before you retaliate and fight.

AMY

Why did you do it? Only God can tell
Such a wonderful person so beautiful as well,
Nobody knows; what was on your mind
But I know; you were lovely and kind.

We used to have little chats and talk about stuff
But I didn't know that something was up,
Whenever I come to work, I miss not seeing you there
Sometimes I look at your spot; I just stand and stare.

I loved your opinions things you had to say
Who would have thought that this could happen? No way

When I heard the news, I just could not believe
I'm so sad; I've lost my wonderful colleague.

RIP Amy wherever you are, I'll always remember you as a shining star.

POEM

I was trying to write you a poem
And had to write it in Braille,
Cos, I know you must be blind
Otherwise our love would not have failed.

I was trying to write you a poem
Then thought words really cannot convey
What I really feel for you
What is there left to say?

SITUATIONSHIP

A situationship I'm told is what many couples have
One partner thinks it's
A relationship and that's what
Makes it sad

The other partner is not clear
They are more confused,
But go through with the relationship
Just to be amused.

There's no respect in this situationship
Just a lot of confusion,
One person gives all the love
The other shows no motivation.

A sexuationship is sex with no ties, together
You're sexual and don't need to tell lies.
You laugh and have casual fun and there's No problem,
when it's done its done.

ATYCHIPHOBIA

Atychiphobia is a fear of failure; it's causing my students to be irregular
They have it in their minds they're going to
fail so most of them don't bother,
(Showing no respect for the teacher)

All year they've worked hard teachers giving them their life
But when it comes to the exams all they do is fuss and strife
Atychiphobia makes them sweat everything
they been taught they forget
(Makes their teachers and parents upset)

Some want to become barbers, or work in kebab shops taking orders
They think it will be an easy life, but life is short, so it helps to be bright
You've been given the chance education is free grab it with both hands
And be happy

Within a year you'll regret not learning
When you realise what you could have been earning
Atychiphobia is not just a word it's in your head
Hope you start revising and forget about street cred.

WHAT IS YOUR COLOUR?

Are you black or are you Caucasian?
Are you Indian or do you call yourself Asian?
There are light skin people who call themselves black
And some black skin people who don't like that.

Mixed race people are usually accepted as black
Some white skin people still put them at the back
I have had many an experience of being called a black B
Or they try to use the N word so eloquently.

MENTO

Mento is a calming place look at me I have a smile on my face
Sit comfortably and relax take in the aroma and have a snack.
A hard day at work? here's what to do come
to Mento they'll de-stress you
Slices of rum cake a cup of coffee from the hills;
beautiful flowers will help you to chill.

While you drink your coffee, you can watch the world go by;
Read or write a novel that brings tears to your eye,
There's a variety of cakes that will make you say hmm,
Mento is the place to be that's true.

If you're just passing by and want to look in
Come look or buy flowers they're so appealing,
But really though I must confess this place is a diamond
With the Finsbury Park address.

Mento is the place to be seen tell all your friends
When they ask where have you been?
Buy flowers or cake take some home for your spouse
Or you can buy and eat in Shhh; there's no need to shout.

EXCELSIOR

I knew that I wanted you from I had the first taste
I knew that I couldn't let any part of you go to waste,
I knew that I'd never let anything of you go in haste
I love the noises that you make.

Your colour is neutral you're not white or brown
Whenever I bite you; put my teeth in you
You make that lovely sound

I've known you from I was young and tasted you then
You've been in many homes everyone's your friend
I've had you with butter I've had you with cheese
I've tried cucumbers on you and even bake beans.

I knew that I wanted you from I had the first bite
I have you in the morning and I have you at night
You come from Jamaica you're such a delight
Excelsior crackers; are my favourite bite.

SORRY

Why say sorry if you keep doing the same thing?
You're saying sorry because you've been caught,
To you it's just a convenience resort
You, telling me sorry don't ease my pain
You're telling me sorry but it's all in vain

You're telling me sorry to make yourself better
I don't want to hear; it really doesn't matter.
I don't like to say sorry unless it's a genuine mistake
Some people say sorry just for their sake.

So please don't patronise me by saying it all the time
To me it's just like you're committing a crime.

IF

If I was in need would you come to my aid?
Would you help me out if I didn't get paid?
If I wanted to talk would you have the time to listen?
Are you the part of my jigsaw that's missing?

Would you tell me off if I made a fool of myself?
Would you leave me if I lost all my wealth?
If I told you I loved you, would you say it back?
If I reached out to touch you would you give me a slap?

Would you still love me if I played the fool?
Or treat me as a child and just say settle and cool.

A POEM FOR MALYNA

Malyna I'll always love you as a brother and a friend
From school days; right to your early end
The Lord wanted you, to do a special job
Your time on earth is done, so we really shouldn't sob

Yes, I cried when I heard the news, I was at a loss
But the tears soon dried up when I realised, you're now with the boss
The people I know; that knew you, have all said good things
And they too like me know that you're now wearing wings

So, until we meet again, you'll forever be in my heart
The way it is at the end is like it was at the start.

RIP Malyna (Martha) Fredricks my dear friend

PEOPLE I LOVE BEING AROUND

I love being around creative and talented people
It makes me creative and talented too
Even at my ripe old age
I'm always learning something new.

Creative and talented people are blessed
I get along with them without stress
So, my talented friends I think you're all great
I'll always support you I won't hesitate

Motivational speaker's youth workers and such
Authors cake makers and painters with brush
Singers, DJ's and actors too I think you're all great
And that's just naming a few.

THE WOMEN

I see women all around; out there crying,
Wondering if their son's coming home or out on the streets dying
Your mother went through pain; to give birth to you,
Now after all these years look what you are putting her through

It's such a shame to see what's happening; from
knife crime you should be refraining
They say its post code wars but for what reason?
Killing your own in the army this would be treason

We'll all die one day but why from the hands of a brother?
God gave us life to live not to kill one another
Is it really that you're bored and have nothing to do?
I can't believe what you're saying or that you believe it too

Do something positive with your life stop the quick money thing
Seems all you want is Versace, Vuitton and Cartier bling
Mothers hearts are breaking about what's happening
Begging for the killings to end because it's very depressing

I see women all around out there crying
Wondering if their sons coming home or out there dying
This affects Mothers, Grandmothers, aunties and sisters too
Their blood is your blood if you get cut their blood drains out too.

THE MEN

Fathers where are you what are you doing?
Where are you when your sons get up in the morning?
Why are you not there; to start the day?
To eat together, bond together come what may.

They need to hear your voice; and points of view
They need guidance and positivity too.
Fathers, Grandfathers uncle and brothers,
This should not be left alone to the mothers.

Fathers, where are you?
What are you doing?
Where are you when your son's gets up in the morning?

THE INCIDENT

The students were on a rampage; today I've seen a different page
Chasing a car down the road because of what someone said.
The students ran riot today well it was more of a frenzy,
Someone didn't like the colour of their skin,
but I think it was more envy.

All they needed to do was listen because they put our lives in danger
Responding to mindless chants from the lips of a racist stranger,
Winding you up just for you to respond it
makes you look worse than they,
People only see and hear you hollowing in the
streets, but they didn't hear what was said

Now let's get our lives back in order it's all about the learning
You didn't follow certain instructions on that
day now that is disconcerting,
Now should we take action for your failure to do as we asked.
We don't blame you for what happened, but you failed to hear our voice

Some of you may have thought you had a good reason
But putting my colleague and your classmate's
life at risk is almost like treason
It was silly what were you going to do?
Ruin your futures because of words from some moronic fools.

BLACKNIFFICENT

Blacknifficent, elaborately infuse with melanin;
And this makes a black person feel great,
We are blacknifficent and this; we should appreciate.
We should use this word to describe how we're feeling
Whenever were feeling good; our soul our mind our body
Happiness running through our blood

I am blacknifficent and I'm so proud
My skin is glowing it stands out in a crowd
I don't need to cover up under a shroud.
Black don't crack I hear this all the time could be the reason
I will read and broaden my mind.

NOTHING ON THE SHELF

It's hard to choose when there's nothing to choose
from; there's nothing on the shelf,
Seems people have gone crazy thinking about themselves.
Suddenly people have money to buy more than they need, is
it because they really want it or is it just blatant greed?

It's sad when I see old people not getting what they want, it's
not that they can't afford it it's just the fact they can't.
Excusez moi s'il vous plait let me speak French,
it seems you don't understand English,
Only two of the same items per customer; or
do you want me to say it in Spanish?

MY GRAVESIDE THOUGHTS

I sit by the graveside I just sit and listen
I look at the flowers; yes, I'm reminiscing
Wondering how? If where and when?
When will I see my parents again?

Nobody knows only god can tell
All I can do is wish them well
I look at the names on the plaque on the wall
I remember when God took them when he gave them the call

I'm sitting by the graveside with tears in my eye
In my head is Why? Why? Why?

MUM 101

Mum if God had wanted you to stay, he would have let you be
You would have been celebrating your hundred and first with me.

But he took you for a reason and only he knows best,
He saw that you were tired, and you needed rest.

But happy birthday mama, I know you're by God's side
It makes me so happy, I feel love and pride.

BROKEN HEART

A heart break is when someone forsake and don't give it it's due
When someone makes you unhappy or say I don't love you, that's true.
When love is only going one way and there's nothing coming back,
You feel you've given everything but now your heart is cracked.

Breaking someone's heart could cause a lot of devastation
It could be the catalyst for many more complications.

MIXED RACE/BLACK

Why is a mixed-race person automatically associated with being black?
The word mix should give you all the facts.
I know they have the features of black people, but their DNA is mixed
So why does everyone play these funny tricks?

I have never heard of a mixed-race person being called white
So, by calling them black does that make it alright?
Megan Markle for instance is getting slaughtered in the press
especially by Piers Morgan, this man I can't digest.

I never hear them say she's white, they always say she's black
And this seems to be the basis for his attacks.
Black people are supportive they take everyone aboard,
Anyway, everyone stems from black, it's there on record.

But still I ask the question why are mixed-race not called white?
Especially by white people, something's just not right
Black people love everyone we always mix and blend
Most young people try to be black; everyone is our friend.

It's all very debatable we can debate until we're blue in the face
Do we call this racism? Is it really about race?
Well I don't know the answer, that's why I put it out there
Does it really matter? Does anyone really care?

IS IT OVER?

I haven't heard of any young boys being stabbed,
Or have they stopped reporting it on the news?
I haven't heard of anyone being stabbed
Since we've all been under this curfew.

Are these boys taking heed to Boris request?
Or are they also confused?
This is an oxymoron,
good bad news

yes, we're under lockdown everyone is staying home
sending messages via mobile phones
making assumptions about the Chinese
and how they have the world on bended knees.

We must be careful of what we're saying
Though we know that the world is decaying,
Everyone is to blame of that there's no doubt
So, mind what you say when you open your mouths.

FRIENDS

I've lost many a dear friend, from the time I've grown
And it just goes to show that you never know
Conroy and Porky were two of the first
Tyrone and Lloyd, is this a curse?

Denise and Deaserie twin girls; who I salute
Rose and Barry who knew each other from youth.
Yvonne and Winston what's going on?
Seems all we have is memories from when we were young.

We've had fun and laughter while growing up
Not realising it could all stop.
As we get older and time runs,
Let's reminisce of days when we were young.

EDUCATION

Education is the key to all success
If you sit down in the classroom and show interest.
You'll learn to be bright in all subjects
Look listen learn and don't mess.

Education is for the strong and the weak
Even if you noisy humble or meek

You can better yourself by doing the do
One plus one equals two,
Alas poor Yorick I knew him well
This is from Hamlet not William Tell,

PANDEMIC

They say this is a third world war and China has won it,
Without firing a single missile, but we're just too blind to see it.
What do we do now? do we just sit and fret?
Or do we get things back in order? we owe the Lord a debt.

Let's change our ways, how we look, speak and treat each other
Because we are all, sisters and brothers
I think God is angry we're tearing his world apart
He wanted us to change so he gave the Chinese the start

Was it just an accident or a sign from God?
I believe he's warning us, so he touched us with the rod
Will we all go back to normal as we were before?
The have all having all and still grabbing more?

The Chinese are getting the blame because that's where it all started
But who on earth can tell? maybe that's what God wanted
To show us that, one stroke can end it all
Look into our lives because we're all heading for a fall.

The world should be a happy place
Where everyone can have fun
Treat each other with respect
Then God's work will be done.

VITAMINS

Vitamins are the source of the day,
Help you work rest and play.

Vitamin A – takes care of my eyes and skin,
Vitamin B – helps me when I'm sleeping,
Vitamin C – fights colds and flu,
So, get plenty that's what you must do.
Vitamin D – strengthen teeth and bones,
You won't be happy when they're all gone.

Iron gives you healthy blood
Protein is good for almost everything
Carbohydrate gives you lots of energy; but make sure it's not stodge
Fibre prevent constipation remove and dislodge.

So, make sure you get your vitamins each day
Long may you work rest and play.

THE AFTERMATH

At the end of all this will I see you again
Will I be able to hug you my friend?
Or will the virus take you away?
Please stay safe I beg and pray.

Will I still be able to look in your eyes?
Laugh with you and get hypnotised
Will I be buying flowers to say bye-bye?
Or shedding tears? I don't want to cry.

Hope we'll be happy, we will meet again
I know where, but I don't know when
So once again; take care, I look forward
To happy times we'll share.

I woke up this morning and there wasn't no pain
Yes! Paracetamol has kicked in again.
Because lately I've been in doubt,
whether to have a lie in bed, or get out,

the pain in my knee has been excruciating
if you've been through it then you'll know what I'm saying
taking tablets is not my thing
I would have preferred, to work it off in the gym.

THANK YOU!

Thanks, to all the friends who have checked up on me;
During this pandemic
Thanks for all your kind words even though it's been
Quite manic

Thanks to the NHS they're giving it a right go,
Trying to save lives, how many? We don't know.
We only hear about, the ones, that have passed away,
But I guarantee they're saving lives every single day.

Some working with and some. without PPE,
So, thanks to all the people who donate to charities.
Thanks to the volunteers, who do it willingly
Taking time out to work voluntarily.

Thanks to all the teachers still, keeping kids in the know,
Thanks to the supermarket workers, trying to get food out on show.
Thanks to the police, who turn up when they're needed,
But no thanks to the people lying in the park sunbathing.

REFLECTION

Let's, all reflect on what we've been through
Where we've been and where we're going to.
What have we done to help the cause?
And did we do it just for applause?

A lot of people have a heart of gold
And some have helped because they've been told
Some people have done it on a whim
Some have jumped in and will sink or swim.

Some of us have lost dear friends, Families, loved ones
but it's not the end,
because in their names we must succeed
we can push forward and still grieve.

Let's treat each other with respect
Help each other don't neglect,
Tell each other that we love and care
They won't hear you when they're not here

ABUSE

Some people are suffering from physical and mental abuse
Even in this pandemic, there's no truce.
The help lines, are doing their best
So, if you can't get through, don't give it a rest. They'll get back to you

FHAP

Florence Hayes Adventure Playground the council took it away,
They shut it down and we wore a frown they said it didn't pay.
Sam and Junior, they were at the helm; keeping it all together
All of us colleagues, sister, brother and friends.

The council decided they wanted to take it
away, so they could save money,
But what about the kids play? Now there isn't any.
The kids would come and have so much fun,
the parents would drop them off,
Even before we were open, at that we all had a laugh.

Kieran, Hazeez, Niassa, Melissa and Bhavita; all part of the crew,
Kingsley, Aisleen, Nina, Brendan and Christina too,
Marcus, Rianna, Scott, Coleen and Evashie. along with Katie and Dom
We would work in the snow, wind, rain or under the blazing sun.

We used to plan adventures and take the kids on retreats
Take them far away from the London streets.
To theme parks and other play groups to mix it up a bit,
The kids showed us all respect; and yes, they enjoyed it.

To these kids we were like mother and father someone they could trust,
We were also their minders, even though some older ones were robust.
Half term was the best times over two hundred kids a day,
FHAP keeping most out of crime; keeping crime at bay.
So why did it have to close? They put the kids out on to the streets,
Also a few of us out of work, now on the streets there's beef.

B.A.M.E

To the black and ethnic minority NHS workers respect due,
A lot of you are dying; but not much is said about you.
You come from all over the world to make the NHS; what it is,
Only to be overlooked and taken for granted.

You love your work, you love your patients, you care and work hard
But it seems you're left behind, there is no regard
You get abuse from a racist few; that you're trying to help
Sometimes the job is dangerous, you try and control yourself

Now more of you are dying,
But they haven't got a clue
They say they're doing tests,
But can we believe, their findings will be true?

WHY?

I don't know why we are not together.
It's a question I ask myself
Because you and I know, we don't want no one else.

Maybe we can't live together but together we can be,
It seems the two of us are blind
Let's open our eyes and see.

Its crazy wasting time like this
When we could be making memories
Why are we looking for perfection?
Putting things in categories.

So, tell me why we're not together
It really doesn't make sense
We will always be a part of each other
Let's stop sitting on the fence.

MUSIC MIX

I don't mind listening to Britney spears, Beyoncé or tears for fears
I don't mind listening to Bob Marley, Chronixx Luciano or Ella Eyre.
Freddie McGregor, Junior Gong, Buju Banton and Biggie Smalls,
A mixture of performers and I like them all.

Chopin, Tchaikovsky and even Brahms and Liszt, I listen
To these also but sometimes I give it a miss.
Queen, Pavarotti and the rolling stones;
sometimes I can't leave them alone

Elvis Pressley, little Richard, from the 50s
The Beatles, the who from the 60s
Marvin Gaye, Tammi Terrell, Ike and Tina Turner
Spandau Ballet, UB40 and Donna Summer.

DONALD TRUMP

You're a racist man Donald and because your name is trump
Every time I hear you speak you give me the flipping hump,
You might be a billionaire you might be rich as muck
But when it comes to getting the black vote mate you're out of luck.

Something is wrong with your equilibrium and its causing others pain
What is wrong with you? You mess up; time and time again
The things you say are meaningless you mess up all the time
If this was on civic street, you'd be arrested for all your crimes.

You control the media that's what you like to do,
You control the rednecks and even Boris Johnson too
You changed everything that Obama set up and think
You should be appreciated, but when the people listen to you
They just get deflated

You might have a pretty wife who dress in fancy clothes
Gucci, Prada, and Ralph Lauren; I suppose
But this does not make a great president
In fact, people hate you even more, you don't
know if you're coming or going
You just don't know the score.
If Gaddafi, Castro, Degulle and Wilson; was alive today
If Mandela, Trudeau and Thatcher were here,
they would have made you pay
You're not a politician, you're a businessman and a clown,
You don't respect anyone; all you do is put people down.

AFTER LOCKDOWN

After lockdown we can do high five. and
pray to God that we're still alive
After lockdown we can play contact sports
and consider, how lives are short.
After lockdown we can see all our mates, look forward to the weekend
And party again.
After lockdown we can go back to the gym,
lift some weights sauna or swim.

After lockdown we can eat out together with sisters, brothers; whoever.
After lockdown we can go on our hols
To Jamaica, Mauritius, or the Costa Del Sol

After lockdown will we still clap on Thursdays. To
show the NHS we still love them truly.
After lockdown let's all live-in peace, let's all live together with dignity.
After lockdown we can go back to churches, Mosques, and temples
We look up to them to set good examples

After lockdown will our lives be blessed.
Will we have learnt anything from the higher being's test?

CORONA

I have a punch bag in my garden I beat it every day
I gave it the name Corona and it must do as I say
The punch bag tries to hit me back when it swings to and fro
But I give it the old one two just to let it know.

I dip slip and slide; to avoid its momentum,
I give it body blows and blows to the head.
I make sure it doesn't get me;
I don't want to be dead.

NATURE

I get a lot of visitors in my garden, they come in of their own free will,
Even in this lockdown, they always come in there still.
I encourage them to come; by laying out food and water,
I know that's what they like; that is what they're after.

I get a lot of visitors in my garden, they come stop, and play
They don't bother me; anyway, what can I say? But hey!
Visitors from different backgrounds, wearing different kinds of armour,
Black, white, red, whatever is there karma.

They never take anything that doesn't belong to them;
they just take what I put out,
They never overstay their welcome, they come in
And then go south.

They bring their own music the sound is wonderful
I'm happy for that; in fact, I'm very grateful,
The birds in my garden I've never seen them fight
They come in and have fun, but where do they go at night?

I CAN'T BREATHE

I lie in my bed and shed a tear; while watching my TV,
What's happening here?
A knee on his neck the man can't breathe.
I'd rather be infected with the corona disease

He can't breathe, he can't breathe,
Now he's stopped breathing,
You've still got your knee on his neck
What is the reason?

Aren't you supposed to try and resuscitate him?
To try and get his heart pumping?
The man is dying and no one's doing nothing

What did he do is he a bomber?
Is he a terrorist or just another; statistic.
This has been going on for ages
And you wonder why people are raging.

I can't imagine how he must have felt
With a knee on his neck and handcuffed as well,
I can't breathe, I can't breathe I heard him utter
While lying on the side of the road, dying in the gutter.

THE SYSTEM

The system is not black, the system is white
How can we infiltrate?
When we try, they say, we exacerbate?

We exacerbate to try to mediate
But no one wants to listen,
Though we know it won't compensate
can we ever debate? And let you be forgiven.

For your intrusion on our lives,
We don't know, but we aim to show,
This isn't simply black or white.

WHAT IS RACISM?

It's hard to explain racism to you; you don't see it, I know that we do,
It's hard to explain day in day out; what racism is all about.
It may be a look it maybe a glare; it maybe a talk it maybe a stare,
It's all the time; but you can't see that, we're
at the end and that's where it's at.

It's an unspoken word it doesn't have to be heard
it's an invisible mist that holds me back, you
don't know; unless you're black.
In my mind I daily struggle; with your unseen chains
There are no words, to describe the pains.

For generations we continue and you;
still don't know what we go through,
The babe in the womb wasn't born to hate,
There are teachings that shapes the way that we're made.

We all have a choice for our sons and daughters
To teach them love and not the opposite,
Ending prejudice is a priority
Stop the violence and the term "minority"

PRAYING FOR LOVE

It's lonely every evening as I walk through my door
I know I say I don't, but I guess I do want more.
I want to be ultra-happy I do have love to give
I have no one to give it to but I must stay positive.

It's hard being a certain age and living on your own
No one to argue with no one to have a moan,
I always seem to give too much; maybe that's where the problem is
I need someone to give the same and not be negative.

Others I know are married and living happily,
So, I must ask myself; what is wrong with me?

THAT STATUE

How many black people pulled that statue down?
It was white people while wearing a frown.
How many black people threw the statue in the sea?
This is something that's puzzling me.

They went there with their ropes and hooks
They had it on their minds,
But when it's a black protest march
Blacks get the blame all the time.

How many black people was spraying graffiti?
No, I don't think it was us,
To say it was would be slander and quite dubious.

Black people are marching; for the murder of
George and to be recognised.
Not to cause destruction and then be categorised

WHAT IS LOVE?

What is love? And how do we say it?
Some people get love and don't even know it.
Some people get love and don't even want it,
Some get love and just abuse it.

What is love? Where does it come from?
From the brain or the heart or just a situation?
Where is love? Because I can't find it
If you got love to give, then please express it

THINKING OF GEORGE

Can you imagine? Now let me check, if
someone had pushed the murderer
Off George Floyd's neck?
Can you imagine how it would have been?
The police would have said they caused a scene.

Can you imagine? Oh; what the heck,
They would have said he was resisting arrest.
Aided and abetted by his saviour,
But no one jumped in; now George is six feet under.

So, two would've been punished; the saviour and George
But George would still be alive without all this rampage
Now he's gone; to him we pay homage

How would it have been if someone had pushed the officer off?
This we'll never know; seems he just lost the plot.

SITTING IN LIMBO (WINDRUSH)

There are marks on the wall where pictures used to hang
But now they're all packed up and sitting in the van.
Sad and broken hearted; look what they done to that man
I'm sitting contemplating; what did he do wrong?
Just a victim of the Windrush situation.

He paid his dues they didn't take that into account
Seems all they wanted was to get him out
He had to prove his kids were his own
Even though they are adults and have now grown.

They locked him up and put him inside
No place to run no place to hide
He couldn't prove his innocence, so this made him cry.

The police treated him as though he was a criminal
The way they acted was inexcusable
He got his passport in the end
But in the meantime, lost time, family and friends.

ACUTE PSYCHOSIS

There's nothing cute; about acute psychosis
In fact, it can damage your brain,
There's nothing cute; about acute psychosis
It can eventually; drive you insane.

Acute psychosis, is a mental state, where
reality can be impaired, it is not cute at all, in fact it should be feared
It is caused by mental illness, such as schizophrenia,
Severe depression; or bipolar disorder.

Heavy and continued use of pot; may not be the cause
But it can make symptoms worse,
And smoking it from an early age
You could make you end up early; in a Herse

I'M FED UP

I'm fed up with people reminding me; about social distancing
I'm fed up with people saying; "stay safe" all the time,
It seems like it's a mantra now and I think it's affecting my mind.
I'm fed up with people saying stay safe; in fact, it's becoming a joke
I don't know who's zooming who? Is it the egg or the yolk?

We're not shaking hands no more; or even giving fist pumps
We're doing the elbow touch even this gives me the hump,
Circumstances with covid19 has changed everything
And though it bothers me; I'm not really complaining.

I know we must be careful so complaining doesn't help,
We have to do what we have to do; everyone got to help themselves

But I'm fed up with people reminding me; about social distancing
I'm fed up of people saying; "stay safe" all the time,
It seems like it's a mantra now and I think it's affecting my mind.

REVERSE ANGLE

Respect my opinions and how I feel; I respect yours let's make this real
You may be black I may be white, why isn't that alright
I've changed things around to create an impression
So, we can get different views of this situation.

Right now, I'm white and I feel privileged; I feel
I could really do some damage.
Now you're black tell me how you feel
Do you feel higher or below me? This is real

You're black walking down the street do you feel free?
I feel good in my new category, when I walk
into a shop no one stand and stare,
When you walk into a shop just you wait and see,
They'll be following your black ass for free.

How does it feel now you're a man of colour
do you feel you have any power?
How does it feel now your skin is dark do you
get nervous walking in the park?
I feel good and I feel free I feel there's no pressure on me
I feel it makes my life easy before it was quite scary

What do you mean you're at the station, are
you catching a train to the pavilion?
What do you mean you were nicked by a
young copper; trying to gain credit?
You said he didn't read you your rights, but he said he read it
You say you're handcuffed and ting; for just
walking the street with your bredrin.

If we could all live for a month in reverse
Take our time to just immerse,
Then we would see just how perverse
The world has become although we're diverse.

FATHER'S DAY

The humble fathers who love their kids; and can't see them
They must believe that they're still wanted,
You've tried but failed and yes, it's sad,
But think of the fathers who walked out; that's bad.

We don't know the reason we don't even care
all we want to know is the love is still there,
how does it feel on a day like this?
Father's Day and you're dismissed

Fathers who love your children I hear your cry
You didn't walk out you didn't say bye-bye,
Circumstances has brought it to this,
You can't see your children and the impact is, it hits.

MENTAL STATE

There's a lot of people with mental health walking on our streets,
No one to help them; so, they give up,
repeat.
There's a lot of people with mental health walking our streets,
No one to help them so they give up;
defeat,

There's a lot of people with mental health walking on our streets,
They are reaching out for help; they get it,
relief.

DON'T PUT FLOWERS

Don't put flowers on my grave put them in my hand
That's the message from me while I'm alive,
Try to understand

Don't go praying for me when I'm gone,
pray for me now
Pray for my life to be blessed,
and for me to find the way how.

Don't put flowers on my grave; put them in my hand
I want to hold and feel them this you must comprehend.
Don't give me praises when I'm gone; tell it to me now
Let me know your feelings let's make this a vow.

THANK YOU!

———————◦———————

Thank you for the time and effort that you put in
Thank you for showing me, the ropes in the gym.
Thank you for giving an old man advise
Thank you for being young and wise.

Thank you for being you and
please don't ever change
if you ever do then
please look at this page.

BLOODLINE

I wish that you were in my bloodline, apart of my family tree
I wish you had my DNA, that part of you would be me.
I have watched you grow from day one, into the flower you are today
Hope I will be part of your life forever; come what may.

You're little now and don't understand what I'm really saying
But as you grow, I hope you'll know and
understand; the love that I'm displaying
You're so cute and joyful, you make everyone smile
They all look at you and say there's a happy child.

Aiyana you're number one, top of my tree
Just like the fairy at Christmas
And that's where you'll always be.

U- TURN FOR MARCUS

Marcus Rashford on his own gave the government a kicking
He told them all; about his humble upbringing,
How his mother struggled to put food on the table
She was young and willing, but she was not able.

The government wanted to take the vouchers away
From the families who needed it most and had no money to pay
He wrote a letter that spelt it out, the vouchers must stay
At first the government 's reply was, no way

Now Boris Johnson has done a U-turn and listened to him keenly
He's decided it's a good idea so this he will do gladly.

BLACK LIVES MATTER

Black lives matter oh yes, we do, black lives matter yes, that's true
Black lives matter what the heck, get your knee off our freeking neck.
Black lives matter let us decide, let your vaccination idea subside
Black lives matter we don't want to try it first
You try it then come tell us the worst.

Your offer epitomises what we say all the time,
We're not animals for you to solve this crime
we are human beings too and don't forget it
black lives matter so don't neglect it.

ATTENTION

Attention is like a currency,
because it is something you must pay.
If you want to be successful
listen to what educators say.
Always do your best and
take in what you're taught,
Absorb all your learning, don't
cut yourself short.

Education is not free,
you must pay, attention,
if you want to develop your mind,
and grow with huge expansion.

FLY-TIPPING

I look out my window in the morning, looking out onto the street
Someone's left an old mattress and some dirty old sheets.
who does this kind of thing? And what time do they do it?
Sometimes you think you know but you just cannot prove it.

Why can't they take it to the dump? that is what I do
The streets are looking so messed up what are they coming to?
Litter tipping is illegal, yes, it is an offence,
the council need to take action
So, they get their comeuppance.

Discarded energy drinks and plastic water bottles
Are filtering onto our streets
Chicken boxes that contains soiled napkins
And uneaten pieces of meat.

I DON'T RELY ON ANYONE

Just like the wind I'm pragmatic;
I move real fast I'm not static
I'm happy as I am doing my own thing,
when you rely on people it's rather draining

their light is red if they stop or say no,
my lights are green and that means go.
So, I won't worry everything is in order,
I give thanks for who I am; to the Father.

WHY ARE WE HATED SO?

why do they hate black people? it's a mystery to me
the Asians hate us, the Chinese hate us with no apology.
white people hate us and all the rest, we even hate ourselves
and can't see that we're blessed.

We need to take control of our own destiny,
let's all read up and teach our families
our history is vast we've been there from creation,
we were once the leaders of the world
but it seems now there is no ambition.

So again, I ask why are we hated so?
we've given you everything; we've given you all our knowledge
you've taken all our bling.

Everyone tries to be like us with fake lips and fake bum
Even your skin colour is fake co.'s you really don't like the sun.
Everyone tries to talk the way we talk but we're not having it,
We've had enough of being ripped off; all this just makes me sick.

In God I trust

PREVIEW

I see things happening in the world, and I try to write and ask questions about them some are serious, some about love, some are a mixture of everyday life as we know and see it today. The poems are amusing and thought provoking, what most people are thinking or saying, some may say they are controversial, but I guarantee they will leave you wanting more.

After my debut book I was asked if my follow up book would be the same? Well I am pleased to say it's better, with the same humour, sarcasm, emotion and points of view.

So many times, people have something to say but find it hard to express their feelings they hold back and implode then later regret that they never said anything, I find putting pen to paper or fingers to keyboard an easier way to express suppressed feelings and what better way to express one's self than with humour, reality and a democratic points of view. Poems of love express what many would like to tell their love ones, and criticism of the not so loved.

I believe in these uncertain times we need to look at life in a different way without holding back, let's face it life is short but maybe we can expand it by looking at it in a different way or from different points of view.